Goodbye, Mayor Menino

by KATHLEEN CHARDAVOYNE

illustrated by CHRISTINE WINSHIP

For all of Boston's children, but especially my sons, Jack and Matthew, who will grow up in a better city because of Mayor Menino.

And for my father, Jack McCarthy, legendary slam poet, who believed that to achieve anything great in life, you have to risk humiliation.

Text copyright © 2013 by Kathleen Chardavoyne
Illustration copyright © 2013 by Christine Winship

ISBN 978-0-615-93804-2

For most American cities
Elected leaders, they come and they go.
They're out of office after a term or two
And leave very little to show.

How different it's been for Boston
Where since 1993
We've had one Thomas Menino
Longest serving mayor in our history.

Mayor Menino, urban mechanic,
Knew how to keep our neighborhoods clean

Trash was picked up, recycling flourished
And look at our parks - they're pristine!

For our mayor it was all about the people
And he could say this with impunity
As he's personally met more than half of Bostonians
And given the rest ample opportunity.

Our mayor would not back down from a challenge
And built up a city to envy

And even amid the world's toughest drivers
He managed to make us bike friendly!

Twenty years in office without the hint of a scandal
What a refreshing and unusual feat!

It may not be so for mayors at posher addresses
But par for the course on Chesterfield Street.

Five terms he's led our great city
Our 53rd mayor so bold

And the only thing he couldn't accomplish
Was a way to prevent growing old.

He leaves behind an inspiring legacy
And a successor schooled on Beacon Hill

Welcome, Mayor Walsh, to City Hall
You've got some huge shoes to fill!

What made him a remarkable leader?
Old fashioned hard work and grit.
Never - no never - did he relent
Nor did he ever take anyone's ... criticism.